D0286488
NEVER ALONE
INTIMATE TIMES WITH JESUS
MARLOWE R. SCOTT

NEVER ALONE

Intimate Times With Jesus

Pearly Gates Publishing LLC, Houston, Texas

Never Alone: Intimate Times With Jesus

ISBN 13: 978-1945117794
ISBN 10: 1945117796
Library of Congress Control Number: 2017945997

For information and bulk ordering, contact:
Pearly Gates Publishing LLC
Angela R. Edwards
P.O. Box 62287
Houston, TX 77205
BestSeller@PearlyGatesPublishing.com

DEDICATION

Never Alone: Intimate Times With Jesus is first dedicated to those who have already experienced the profound messages and peace found while personally spending quality time with God and the Scriptures.

Secondly, it is dedicated to all who seek to apply the message of this book to their spiritual walk and growth in our Savior, Jesus Christ.

Finally, to all nature lovers who appreciate and seek to properly use and preserve God's creation that He prepared for mankind, this is also dedicated to you.

ACKNOWLEDGEMENTS

First, to Almighty God: To Him be all glory and praise for the blessings, gifts, and wisdom He has given me to witness through writing and poetry. I am humbled by the many inspirations given to me and pray they are conveyed clearly and are spiritually-nourishing to those who read them.

Secondly, to my daughter, Angela R. Edwards: She has allowed God to use her talents. As CEO, Editor-in-Chief, and Publisher of Pearly Gates Publishing LLC, she always produces my writings to perfection. I truly thank God for YOU!

PREFACE

The thought and desire to write another book was **not** on my agenda; *however,* God had other plans. He has gifted and blessed me in so many ways, it is hard ***not*** to write and encourage others. Inspiration for *Never Alone: Intimate Times With Jesus* comes from many sources: my family background, love of nature and God's creation in general, as well as many hours alone spent reading, singing, and remembering days gone by.

As someone attending church since infancy and my mother being a soloist and Senior Choir President, I, as a child, accompanied her to many rehearsals and events. My memory overflows with hymns, gospel, and spiritual songs - and each of my books includes a few. I was even inspired to write a poem entitled *Songs in the Night* that is found in my first book, *Spiritual Growth: From Milk to Strong Meat.*

To share more about my country girl farm life:

- My mother sewed, crocheted, and canned the foods raised or purchased for the Winter.
- My father grew a variety of vegetables to include beans, onions, cabbage, lettuce, and okra to name a few.
- Uncle Harry lived on an apple and peach orchard farm, and I still remember the tasty, fresh fruits and apple cider in the Fall.
- Uncle Leon lived on a dairy farm, and there was always fresh milk to take home with cream floating on the top when we visited.
- Uncle Clarence was a mechanic and became a minister who our former pastor, Rev. Richard W. Jones, knew in Cape May, New Jersey.
- Aunt Jennie was married to Uncle Herman Williams, and he worked at a butcher meat-packing house. He would come butcher our hogs and have their meat smoked. The smell was awesome when the meat came home to hang in our cellar.

I **love** animals, especially dogs, and have made "pets" of many of God's creatures. I enjoy the colorful birds chirping as they greet me in the morning and, as well, before they turn in for the night. Colorful butterflies flit among the blossoms, and woodpeckers run up and down tree limbs while enjoying the suet I put out in the Winter. As a child, I made pets of almost *anything*, including a large, white leghorn hen named "Beducks" that would lay double-yolk eggs on a regular basis.

My current yard has seen deer, squirrels, chipmunks, rabbits, wild turkeys, turtles, opossum, and even baby skunks!

One day, I was looking out the kitchen window and saw a black bird perched on the edge of the basin of water set out for them to drink. He seemed intent on drinking; however, a few moments later, he lifted up his head and in his mouth was a piece of bread that had hardened in the sun. That smart bird had the sense to soften the bread with water, as he then placed it on the ground and bit it into small pieces so he could eat! Just think: Growing up, people were teased about being a 'bird brain'! Well, **that** bird seemed very intelligent to me! God's Word tells us that He provides food for the birds, so why not mankind?

****

There is a hymn I learned as a child written by Cecil Frances Alexander. The title is *All Things Bright and Beautiful*. It starts with singing the refrain:

REFRAIN:
All things bright and beautiful,
All creatures great and small,
All things wise and wonderful;
The Lord God made them all.

Each little flower that opens,
Each little bird that sings,
God made their glowing colors.
God made their tiny wings.

The purple-headed mountain,
The river running by,
The sunset, and the morning
That brightens up the sky.

The cold wind in the Winter,
The pleasant Summer sun,
The ripe fruits in the garden;
God made them, every one.

God gave us eyes to see them,
And lips that we might tell
How great is God Almighty,
Who has made all things well.

HALLELUJAH, HALLELUJAH!
PRAISES TO GOD THE FATHER, GOD THE SON,
AND THE PRECIOUS HOLY SPIRIT!

INTRODUCTION

My God-directed purpose is to *first* share my experiences and blessings in an effort to encourage and nourish others by sharing personal testimonies through scripture, stories, and poetry. *Secondly,* I am to plant spiritual seeds which develop into the unsaved receiving salvation by accepting Jesus Christ as their personal Savior - and helping the already saved to continually grow.

Before sharing and moving forward with this book, I would like to say something about the title.

Everyone has times of being alone, and I (like many) have a lot of "alone" time. During these times of peace and quiet, I am afforded time to read scriptures and inspirational books, write poetry, and other literary pursuits. The word "intimate" is the sharing of a close, personal relationship with someone, such as a family member or friend. As a ***Christian,*** my best friend of all is Jesus Christ, as He truly walks and talks with me! During these times, I often have to pray like David in Psalm 51:10:

"*Create in me a clean heart, O God; and renew a right spirit within me.*"

What a blessing!

There are a variety of reasons why an individual may be alone. Whatever that reason may be, a Christian **MUST** realize that being one of God's own, time must be spent in worship, study, and prayer on a regular and individual basis. There are retreats - personal and group - which have deeply-impacted and enriched my Christian growth and took my devotion and love of Jesus Christ to a higher level.

I am a morning person (so to speak). My energy level is higher, and my mind and soul fresh for a new day. I praise God for yet *another* day's journey, and the following passage of scripture fits right in for me:

"*It is of the LORD's mercies that we are not consumed, because His compassions fail not. They are new every morning; great is thy faithfulness.*"

Lamentations 3:22-23

The hymn *Great is Thy Faithfulness* is based on that scripture. The author is Thomas O. Chisholm. The second verse of this inspiring hymn is:

"*Summer and Winter and Springtime and harvest,*
Sun, moon, and stars in their courses above
Join with all nature I manifold witness
To thy great faithfulness, mercy, and love."

As you read this book, you will find other hymns that have enriched my spiritual life. It is my prayer that they do the same for yours.

At the end of the book are questions to consider and places for you to journal your thoughts and responses.

TABLE OF CONTENTS

CHAPTER ONE

At the beginning of 2017, I committed to reading a book by Peggy Joyce Ruth titled *Psalm 91: God's Umbrella of Protection*. How many know that some of the best things in life **ARE** free? That precious little book was a ***free gift*** included in a gift package from a church event. It contains many true testimonies about how the Psalm protected and blessed many. It is highly recommended for those who want not only evidence, but also ways to incorporate Psalm 91 into their lives.

Testimonies from the book are real and life-changing, showing the power in knowing and applying God's Word. Some of those testimonies are:

- A missionary in Africa prayed during shootings and raid in a village. Although killings, beatings, and robbery occurred, the place where the missionary was located was untouched - an area which contained considerable resources and money.
- Some individuals were afforded protection during tornadoes and other disastrous situations.
- One entire military unit memorized and recited Psalm 91 daily during wartime, and **ALL** returned home safely.
- There are also stories of miraculous healings for medical situations - ones the physicians had given up on.

If you do not have a favorite memory scripture, I suggest you read and pray over Psalm 91. I read and listen to it daily on my Bible app.

Note: Even Satan the deceiver quoted part of Psalm 91:11,12 in his temptation of Jesus (as recorded in Matthew 4:6). *He left out the assurance found in the words, "...to keep thee in all thy ways..."*

For me, being alone, thinking about familiar scriptures, and enjoying the sunrise and nature in general brings a deep sense of peace. Creative thoughts, ideas, childhood memories, and special occasions often flood my mind. At those times, feelings of deep, inner peace, unexplainable joy, and comfort come over me.

In these senior years, God has blessed me to write Christ-centered books and inspirational poems. My very first poem was written in the mid-1990s. It is entitled *Jesus, My Friend Jesus*. There are five verses, two which are shared here:

VERSE 1:

What a friend we have in Jesus;
He all our sins and griefs will bear.
Our Friend Jesus came and left Someone special
When He ascended to His Father in the air!

VERSE 5:

Come quickly! Praise and celebrate with me
A Friend who loves unconditionally,
without compare;
His Name is Emanuel - Wonderful Jesus;
be ye ready to meet Him
When He comes again from Glory -
shouting through the air!

The entire poem is included in my first book, *Spiritual Growth: From Milk to Strong Meat.*

Other book titles are *Believing Without Seeing: The Power of Faith; Keeping It Real: The Straight and Narrow;* and a trilogy encompassing all three books, *Worth the Journey: The Train Ride to Glory*. All four books have earned the recognition of Best-Seller on Amazon.

While I was on vacation in the mountains, gazing out on the patio, the inspiration came in a flash! God gave me the poem, *Abuse is Not Love,* in a matter of **minutes** on my 71st birthday. The first verse is shared here:

"Abuse comes in many forms.
In some cultures and homes,
Abuse is the norm.
It's directed at children and adults, too;
Has abuse ever happened to you?"

Abuse is Not Love has become the staple poem for the *God Says I am Battle-Scar Free* book series. Angela R. Edwards, Best-Selling Author and CEO of Pearly Gates Publishing, LLC of Houston, Texas is the Founder of the Battle-Scar Free Movement, and many lives are being changed through the ministry of the books.

CHAPTER TWO

I *love* music, especially the hymns I grew up learning and singing in the Methodist church. One comes to mind about being alone with Jesus Christ. The author is G.T. Byrd:

ON MOUNT OLIVE'S SACRED BROW

On Mount Olive's sacred brow

Jesus spent the night in pray'r.

He's the pattern for us all, all alone,

If we'll only steal away

In some portion of the day,

We will find it always pays to be alone.

REFRAIN:

There are times I'd like to be

All alone with Christ my Lord.

I can tell Him of my troubles all alone.

There are times I'd like to be

All alone with Christ my Lord.

I can tell Him of my troubles all alone.

There are times I'd like to be
With the sanctified and blest.
There are times I like to be all alone,
God can always grace impart,
To my weary, saddened heart.
There are times I'd like to be just all alone.

There are days to fast and pray
For the pilgrim in his way.
There are days to be with Christ all alone,
We can tell Him all our grief.
He will give us quick relief.
There are times I'd like to be just all alone.

When a heart is broken up
With a tearful, lonesome cup,
Then's the time to go to Christ all alone.
In our blessed Lord divine,
There is peace and joy sublime
When we take our sorrows all to Him alone.

Richard Smallwood composed a soul-stirring song that aptly tells my personal testimony! Countless choirs have ministered mightily through its words and beautiful melody. I personally often tear up when praising and singing the following song:

JESUS, YOU'RE THE CENTER OF MY JOY

CHORUS:
Jesus, You're the center of my joy.
All that's good and perfect comes from You.
You're the heart of my contentment,
Hope for all I do;
Jesus, You're the center of my joy.

When I've lost my direction,
You're the compass for my way.
You're the fire and light
When nights are long and cold;
In sadness, You're my laughter
That shatters all my fears.
When I'm all alone, Your hand is there to hold.

You are why I find pleasure

In the simple things in life.

You're the music in the meadows and the streams,

The voices of the children, my family, and my home.

You're the source and finish of my highest dreams.

****

On the cover, you see a picture of a gazebo. That entire set of imagery is much like the one I have in my yard. There is a calm breeze that passes out there, and the birds chirp in the trees and bushes that surround the gazebo constantly. From the serenity of that scene, I also see birds building nests, rabbits hopping, and chipmunks darting in and out of the shrubbery and plants. It is peaceful and restful to my soul, and I receive many inspirations while gazing around the natural beauty of the back yard. Also out there, I often remember some of the many songs that have blessed and encouraged my soul; *Precious Memories* is such a hymn.

PRECIOUS MEMORIES

By Authors J.B.F. Wright and Lonnie B. Combs

CHORUS:

Precious memories; how they linger,

How they ever flood my soul.

In the stillness of the midnight,

Precious sacred scenes unfold.

Precious memories, unseen angels,

Sent from somewhere to my soul;

How they linger, ever near me,

And the sacred past unfolds.

Precious father, loving mother;

Fly across the lonely years.

And old home scenes of my childhood

In fond memory appears.

I remember Mother praying;

Father, too, on bended knee.

The sun is sinking, shadows falling,

But their prayers still follow me.

CHAPTER THREE

There are many instances in the scriptures where people were alone with God or when other significant situations occurred.

- Jesus went alone to pray at Gethsemane before His crucifixion. It was a time of great mental and spiritual suffering for Him, yet He endured it for you and me.
- Moses went on Mount Sinai alone to receive the 10 Commandments from God.
- Daniel openly petitioned God, even when a decree went out not to do so.
- John, while on the island of Patmos, received many revelations recorded in the Book of Revelation. For example, Revelation 1:9 reads, "*I, John, your brother and fellow partaker in the tribulation and kingdom and perseverance which are in Jesus, was on the island called Patmos because of the Word of God and the testimony of Jesus*".

Recently, an inspiring movie was produced by Stephen Kendrick and Gary Wheeler entitled *War Room.* It was widely acclaimed and viewed by Christians because it clearly demonstrated the value and need for prayer in our lives. Another bright spot in the movie is that lives were turned around and the young daughter learned to follow her mother's example. She had some of her childish desires fulfilled, especially on the family level!

Many today may have a "Prayer Room" or "Prayer Closet". Others choose a quiet place and record their prayers in a journal and then write the result when it occurs.

Prayer is the way - the "key", if you will - we communicate with our Heavenly Father and Jesus Christ. The Holy Bible documents a prayer life for His people in both the Old and New Testaments.

Although trials and problems will surely come, the comfort in knowing that praying to God is His will for our lives will be a blessing. It shows that God not only cares, but knows what is best for His children.

"But thou, when you prayest, enter into thy closet, and when thou hast shut thy door, pray to thy Father which is in secret; and thy Father which seeth in secret shall reward thee openly"

(Matthew 6:6).

Following are a few scriptures further supporting the need to be alone and have an active prayer life:

- Genesis 32:24 - "Then Jacob was left alone, and a man wrestled with him until daybreak."
- Matthew 14:43 - "After He had sent the crowds away, He went up on the mountain by Himself to pray; and when it was evening, He was there alone."
- Matthew 26:39 - "And He went a little beyond them, and fell on His face and prayed, saying, 'My Father, if it is possible, let this cup pass from Me; yet not as I will, but as You will'."
- Mark 1:35 - "In the early morning, while it was still dark, Jesus got up, left the house, and went away to a secluded place, and was praying there."

- Mark 6:45-46 - "Immediately, Jesus made His disciples get into the boat and go ahead of Him to the other side of Bethsaida, while He Himself was sending the crowd away. After bidding them farewell, He left for the mountain to pray."
- Luke 4:42 - "When day came, Jesus left and went to a secluded place; and the crowds were searching for Him, and came to Him and tried to keep Him from going away from them."
- Luke 5:15-16 - "But the news about Him was spreading even farther, and large crowds were gathering to hear Him and to be healed of their sicknesses. But Jesus Himself would often slip away to the wilderness to pray."
- Luke 6:12 - "It was at this time that He went off to the mountain to pray, and He spent the whole night in prayer to God."

****

The following hymn is another inspiring, true message concerning the most important things in order to have a quality Christian walk and testimony for the world to see. This is yet another song I can vividly still hear my mother sing!

****

YES, CHRIST IS ALL

By Author Kenneth Morris

I don't possess houses or lands,
fine clothes or jewelry;
Sorrows and cares in this old world,
my lot seems to be.
But I have a Christ, who paid the price
way back on Calvary,
And Christ is all, all in all this world to me.

CHORUS:

Yes, Christ is all; He's everything to me.

Yes, Christ is all; He rules the land and sea.

Yes, Christ is all; without Him, nothing could be.

Christ is all, all in all this world to me.

There are some folk who look and

long for this world's riches.

There are some folk who look

for power, position, too.

But I have a Christ all in my life;

this makes me happy.

For Christ is all, all and all this world to me.

Yes, Christ is all; means more to me

than this world's riches.

He is my sight, my guiding light

through pathless seas.

Yes, it's mighty nice to own a Christ

who will my Friend be.

Yes, Christ is all, all and all this world to me.

CHAPTER FOUR

Digging Deeper in Scripture

There are numerous ways to study and learn how to apply scriptures to our daily lives. Careful study and Bible helps are available for this purpose. During times of our personal trials, doubts, hurts, temptations, and low points in life, memorization of scripture is very helpful.

In the first chapter, it was shared how Satan left out important words in Psalm 91. Following are a few other scriptures often quoted, but the full context and meaning are not fully revealed.

Biblical promises are often committed to memory by Christians, such as those which follow. *However*, before declaring the right to the promises in scripture, we must know the **full** context and meaning of a passage…not just one part.

1. For example, Romans 8:28 is probably one of the most familiar: "And we know that all things work together for good to them that love God, to them who are called according to His purpose." What does "...to them who are called according to His purpose" mean?

2. Another to consider and explore is Luke 6:38. "Give, and it shall be given unto you; good measure, pressed down, and shaken together, and running over, shall men give into your bosom. For with the same measure that ye mete withal it shall be measured to you again." How often do we consider the second sentence of this quote? How does this impact what you give and receive?

3. One of my favorites is Matthew 6:33. "But seek ye first the kingdom of God, and His righteousness; and all these things shall be added unto you." It is necessary to read scripture verses before this quote to know what the things added are. Take time to write them here.

CONCLUSION

It is my sincerest desire that the messages of this book, along with songs with deep meaning, enrich your spiritual walk with Jesus. I have found joy, contentment, and inner peace through my times of being alone with **my** Friend, *Jesus*! May you also find this to be true (or come true) in your life while here on Earth.

Additionally, I pray the inspired poems from the Holy Spirit will provide not only comfort, but that their messages will point you to our Savior and those things that intimate times with Jesus can bring to your life as well.

In these rapidly-changing times of technological advances, microwave society, and need for speed, we **MUST** remember an important verse - one which I firmly believe:

"*Christ is the same yesterday and today and forever*"

(Hebrews 13:8).

In summary, I can humbly say that my senior years have become rewarding not only for me, but for others who have shared how my God-inspired books have positively influenced and changed their lives. It is gratifying to look back over my life and share the stories while encouraging others to join this Christian journey.

TO GOD BE THE GLORY!

JOURNAL DURING YOUR INTIMATE TIMES WITH JESUS

How do you spend intimate times with Jesus?

What time of day is best for **YOU** to have intimate times with Jesus in prayer and devotion?

Where is your favorite place to be alone with Jesus?

How have hymns, spiritual music, and poems inspired, comforted, and guided you?

INSPIRATIONAL POEMS BY MARLOWE R. SCOTT

Jesus, My Friend Jesus

Kinship Benefits

Songs in the Night

Higher Spiritual Heights

The Sheepfold

Growing in Faith

Abuse is Not Love

Calvary's Cross

The Announcement

BEST-SELLING TITLES BY MARLOWE R. SCOTT

Spiritual Growth: From Milk to Strong Meat
© 2015

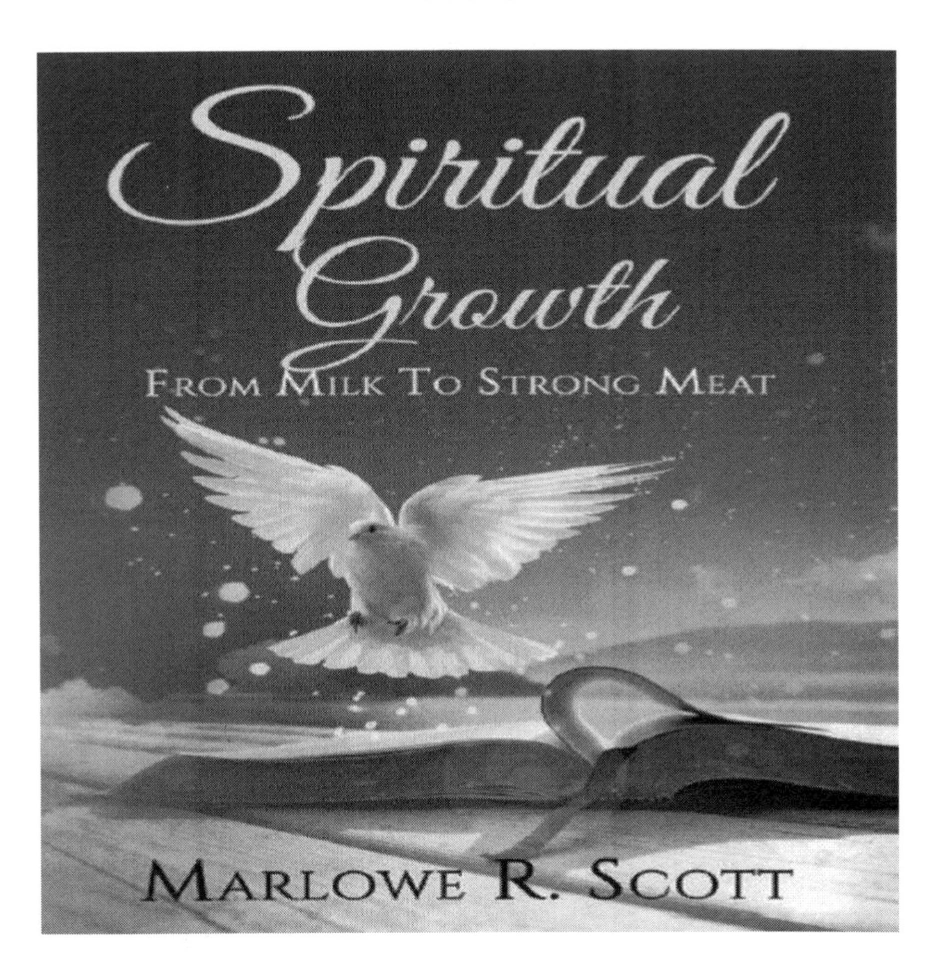

Visit www.PearlyGatesPublishing.com

or other online retailers to purchase.

Believing Without Seeing: The Power of Faith
© 2015

Visit www.PearlyGatesPublishing.com

or other online retailers to purchase.

Keeping It Real: The Straight and Narrow
© 2016

Visit www.PearlyGatesPublishing.com

or other online retailers to purchase.

Worth the Journey: The Train Ride to Glory
© 2016

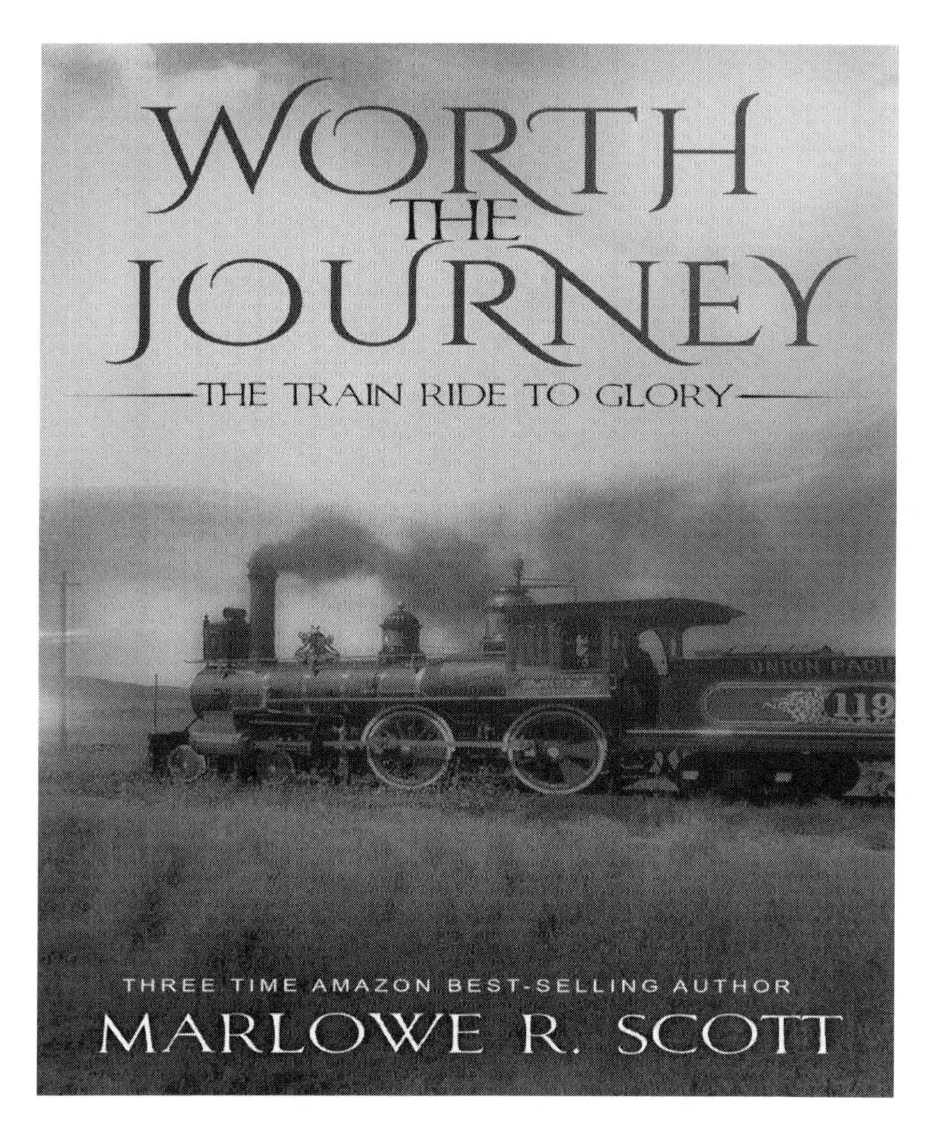

Visit www.PearlyGatesPublishing.com

or other online retailers to purchase.

ABOUT THE AUTHOR

Marlowe R. Scott was born at home in a small, South Jersey community of Cedarville, New Jersey. Her parents were Carl and Helena Harris. Marlowe is a true country girl who loves nature - God's wondrous creation. She enjoys seeing birds preparing nests, wild turkeys roaming the backyard with their young, and the stately deer in the field and property tree line where she lives in Browns Mills, New Jersey.

Marlowe has been blessed with many talents. They include: writing, poetry, music, sewing, crocheting, quilting, and floral designs. Her educational focus was the Communication Arts Degree Program at Burlington County College, as well as attendance and participation in numerous government-sponsored training venues.

Marlowe's extensive experiences encompassed duties as: Leadership, Education, and Development Facilitator; Equal Employment Opportunity Counselor; Quality Management Facilitator; and member of the New Jersey Quality Board of Examiners. With her commitment to quality, she also participated in videoconferences, workshops, and community volunteer activities.

One highlight of her career was a conference held in Baltimore, Maryland where she was a member of a select group of individuals who met and interacted with Retired U.S. Army General and Former U.S. Secretary of State, Colin Powell. Marlowe retired after 33 years of dedicated federal civil service.

She has taught Floral Arts and Crafts in adult education, won ribbons for her creative designs, and appeared on television. Currently, she devotes most of her time to quilting and developing her home-based business, M.R.S. Inspirations, with the motto "Magnificent Revelations Are My Specialty". Her creations are focused on making special memories in lap quilts, throws, baby quilts, and pillows which show love and give comfort to the recipient.

Readers of her books have verbally expressed, as well as given written endorsements and testimonies, sharing how they were inspired, experienced spiritual growth, and comfort through her writing and poems. She also received commendation from former U.S. President Barack Obama and family for sharing with them *Spiritual Growth: From Milk to Strong Meat.*

Marlowe is married to Andrew Scott and has three children: Carl, James, and Angela, as well as five grandchildren and a host of great-grandchildren. She is currently a member of Tabernacle Baptist Church, Burlington, New Jersey.